# Jagoe Surname

# Ireland: 1600s to 1900s

From Ireland Church Records of Baptism, Marriage and Death

Comprised of Roman Catholic and Church of Ireland Records

From Counties Carlow, Cork, Kerry and Dublin City

Compiled by **Donovan Hurst**

March 12, 2012

ISBN: 0985134364
ISBN-13: 978-0-9851343-6-5

# Dedication

This work is dedicated to all of those that came before us and shaped our lives to make us the people that we are today.

# Table of Contents

# Introduction

This is a compilation of individuals who have the surname of Jagoe that lived in the country of Ireland from the 1600s to the 1900s. I have placed each entry into one of four categories: Families, Individual Births/Baptisms, Individual Burials, and Individual Marriages. If a marriage entry primarily concerns an Individual Jagoe who is female, then I have placed that entry under the category of Individual Marriages. If a marriage entry primarily concerns an Individual Jagoe who is male, then I have placed that entry under the category of Families. Images of many of these listings are available at http://churchrecords.irishgenealogy.ie/churchrecords/.

To help guide the reader of this work, the format of this book is as follows:

- Main Family Entry (Husband and Wife) (Father and Mother)

  o Child of Main Family Entry, including Spouse(s) when available

    ▪ Grandchild of Main Family Entry, including Spouse(s) when available

      • Great-Grandchild of Main Family Entry, including Spouse(s) when available

(Bolded Text) following any entry includes any additional information such as Residence(s), Occupation(s), Signature(s), etc. when available.

# Hurst

Some of the fonts used in this work symbolizes Celtic writing. The traditional letters, numbers, and punctuation marks and their Celtic counterparts are as follows:

Traditional Letters (Uppercase & Lowercase)

A a B b C c D d E f G g H h I i J j K k L l M m N n O o P p Q q R r S s T t U u V v W w X x Y y Z z

Celtic Letters (Uppercase & Lowercase)

A a B b C c D ð E e F f G g H h I i J j K k L l M m

N n O o P p Q q R r S s T t U u V v W w X x Y y Z z

Traditional Numbers

1 2 3 4 5 6 7 8 9 10

Celtic Numbers

1 2 3 4 5 6 7 8 9 10

Traditional Punctuation

. , : ' " & - ( )

Celtic Punctuation

. , : ' " & - ( )

# Jagoe Surname Ireland: 1600s to 1900s

# Parish Churches
# Cork & Ross
# (Roman Catholic or RC)

Ballinhassig Parish, Bandon Parish, Bantry Parish, Clonakilty Parish, Cork - South Parish, Cork - SS. Peter & Paul Parish, Drimoleague Parish, Dunmanway Parish, Enniskeane Parish, Innishannon Parish, Kilbrittain Parish, Kilmacabea Parish, Kilmichael Parish, Kilmurry Parish, Kilmurry, Moviddy, Kilbonane, & Cannavee Parish, Kinsale Parish, Muintervara Parish, Skibbereen & Rath Parish, Skibbereen (Creagh & Sullon) Parish, and Tracton Abbey Parish.

# Dublin (Church of Ireland)

Beggar's Bush Barracks Parish, Grangegorman Parish, Kilmainham Parish, St. Andrew Parish, St. George Parish, St. John Parish, St. Jude Parish, St. Luke Parish, St. Matthias Parish, St. Nicholas Within Parish, St. Peter Parish, and St. Werburgh Parish.

# Dublin (Roman Catholic or RC)

St. Andrew Parish and St. Mary, Pro Cathedral Parish.

# Kerry (Roman Catholic or RC)

Tralee Parish.

# Families

- Abraham Jagoe & Julia Harris

  ○ John Jagoe – bapt. 20 Oct 1816 (Baptism, **Skibbereen (Creagh & Sullon) Parish (RC)**)

  ○ Patrick Jagoe – bapt. 30 May 1819 (Baptism, **Skibbereen (Creagh & Sullon) Parish (RC)**)

  ○ William Jagoe – bapt. 18 Nov 1821 (Baptism, **Skibbereen (Creagh & Sullon) Parish (RC)**)

  ○ Thomas Jagoe – bapt. 25 Jul 1824 (Baptism, **Skibbereen (Creagh & Sullon) Parish (RC)**)

**Abraham Jagoe (father):**

**Residence - Gortnaclohe - October 20, 1816**

**November 18, 1821**

**July 25, 1824**

- Abraham Jagoe & Mary Walsh

  ○ Ellen Jagoe – bapt. 16 Dec 1821 (Baptism, **Kilmichael Parish (RC)**)

  ○ Margaret Jagoe – bapt. 28 May 1824 (Baptism, **Drimoleague Parish (RC)**)

  ○ William Jagoe – bapt. 26 Sep 1826 (Baptism, **Drimoleague Parish (RC)**)

- B. H. Jagoe & Unknown

  ○ Sarah Amelia Jagoe & John Symons – 14 Jun 1887 (Marriage, **St. Matthias Parish**)

**Signatures:**

# Hurst

Sarah Amelia Jagoe (daughter):

    Residence - 3 Hatch Street, Dublin & Macroom, Co. Cork - June 14, 1887

John Symons, son of John Symons (son-in-law):

    Residence - 13 North Parade Penzance, Cornwall - June 14, 1887

    Occupation - Surgeon - June 14, 1887

John Symons (father):

    Occupation - Chemist

B. H. Jagoe (father):

    Occupation - Surgeon

Wedding Witnesses:

Henry Jagoe & Mary L. Jagoe

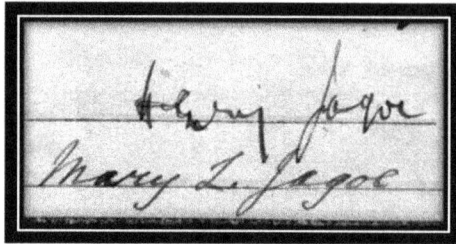

Signatures:

- Charles Jagoe & Elizabeth Jagoe

    - John Henry Jagoe – b. 17 May 1854, bapt. 21 Aug 1854 (Baptism, Grangegorman Parish)

Charles Jagoe (father):

    Residence - 9 Royal Canal Terrace - August 21, 1854

    Occupation - Shop Keeper - August 21, 1854

- Charles Jagoe & Ellen Dawley – 24 Jan 1839 (Marriage, Bantry Parish (RC))

- Charles Jagoe & Honora Burke

    - Mary Jagoe – bapt. 21 Sep 1834 (Baptism, Kilmacabea Parish (RC))

- Charles Jagoe & Nancy Kingston

    - Mary Jagoe – bapt. 21 Dec 1817 (Baptism, Drimoleague Parish (RC))

# Jagoe Surname Ireland: 1600s to 1900s

- Christopher Jagoe & Ellen Gennings

  - John Jagoe – bapt. 20 Jun 1824 (Baptism, **Cork - South Parish (RC)**)

- Doctor Jagoe & Margaret Cunningham

  - Catherine Jagoe – bapt. 16 May 1852 (Baptism, **Clonakilty Parish (RC)**)

## Doctor Jagoe (father):
### Residence - W House - May 16, 1852

- Edward Jagoe & Ellen Russell

  - Elizabeth Jagoe – bapt. 9 Mar 1820 (Baptism, **Dunmanway Parish (RC)**)

## Edward Jagoe (father):
### Residence - Pookeen - March 9, 1820

- Elijah Jagoe & Jane Flinn – Apr 1808 (Marriage, **St. Mary, Pro Cathedral Parish** (RC))

  - Thomas Jagoe – bapt. 7 Jul 1811 (Baptism, **St. Mary, Pro Cathedral Parish** (RC))

- Henry Jagoe & Eleanor Unknown

  - Thomas Jagoe – bapt. 30 Jan 1685 (Baptism, **St. John Parish**)

  - Jo Jagoe (son) – bapt. 14 Oct 1688 (Baptism, **St. John Parish**)

  - William Jagoe – bapt. 5 Apr 1691 (Baptism, **St. John Parish**), bur. 1 Jun 1698 (Burial, **St. John Parish**)

  - Henry Jagoe – b. 10 Mar 1693, bapt. 12 Mar 1693 (Baptism, **St. John Parish**)

  - Robert Jagoe – b. 14 Apr 1696, bapt. 19 Apr 1696 (Baptism, **St. John Parish**), bur. 20 Jul 1697 (Burial, **St. John Parish**)

  - Mary Jagoe – b. 1697, bapt. 16 Aug 1702 (Baptism, **St. John Parish**)

  - Eleanor Jagoe – b. 7 Oct 1698, bapt. 12 Oct 1698 (Baptism, **St. John Parish**), bur. 27 Dec 1698 (Burial, **St. John Parish**)

  - Eleanor Jagoe – bapt. 14 Nov 1699 (Baptism, **St. John Parish**), bur. 4 Jun 1712 (Burial, **St. John Parish**)

# Hurst

- o Mary Jagoe – b. 21 Mar 1701, bapt. 23 Mar 1701 (Baptism, **St. John Parish**)

Henry Jagoe (father):

Residence - Woodkey - April 19, 1696

October 12, 1698

November 14, 1699

March 23, 1701

August 16, 1702

Occupation - Garbertman - April 19, 1696

October 12, 1698

November 14, 1699

March 23, 1701

August 16, 1702

- Henry Jagoe & Ellen Barry (B a r r y) – 11 Nov 1841 (Marriage, **Dunmanway Parish** (RC))

  - o Henry Jagoe – bapt. 28 Jan 1843 (Baptism, **Dunmanway Parish** (RC))

  - o John Jagoe – bapt. 19 Jan 1847 (Baptism, **Dunmanway Parish** (RC))

Henry Jagoe (father):

Residence - Mulane - November 11, 1841

Pookeen - January 28, 1843

Ellen Barry (mother):

Residence - Mulane - November 11, 1841

January 19, 1847

- Henry Jagoe & Sarah Taylor – 29 Oct 1714 (Marriage, **St. John Parish**)

  - o John Jagoe – bapt. 24 Oct 1718 (Baptism, **St. Luke Parish**)

Henry Jagoe (father):

Occupation - Poddle Joiner - October 24, 1718

Sarah Taylor (mother):

Relationship Status at Marriage - widow

# Jagoe Surname Ireland: 1600s to 1900s

- Henry Jagoe & Sarah Unknown

  - Sodwich Jagoe – bapt. 14 Nov 1726 (Baptism, **St. Werburgh Parish**)

  - Hester Jagoe – bapt. 1728 (Baptism, **St. Werburgh Parish**), bur. 27 Oct 1728 (Burial, **St. Werburgh Parish**)

  - William Jagoe – bapt. 27 Sep 1729 (Baptism, **St. Werburgh Parish**)

  - Edward Jagoe – bapt. 2 Jan 1730 (Baptism, **St. Werburgh Parish**)

  - John Jagoe – bur. 20 May 1731 (Burial, **St. Werburgh Parish**)

**John Jagoe (son):**

**Age at Death - Infant**

  - Samuel Jagoe – bapt. 1 May 1735 (Baptism, **St. Werburgh Parish**)

**Henry Jagoe (father):**

**Residence - Warburgh's Street - November 14, 1726**

**1728**

**September 27, 1729**

**January 2, 1730**

**Cork Hill - May 1, 1735**

- Henry Jagoe & Unknown

  - William Jagoe – bur. 14 Jul 1732 (Burial, **St. Werburgh Parish**)

**William Jagoe (son):**

**Age at Death - infant**

**Henry Jagoe (father):**

**Residence - Coal Alley - July 14, 1732**

# Hurst

- Henry Couch Jagoe & Sarah Anne Jagoe

  o Lucy Amelia Jagoe – b. 3 Dec 1864, bapt. 12 Mar 1865 (Baptism, **Kilmainham Parish**) (Baptism,

    **St. Jude Parish**)

  o Charles Albert Jagoe – b. 7 Nov 1866, bapt. 11 Dec 1866 (Baptism, **Kilmainham Parish**)

    (Baptism, **St. Jude Parish**)

**Henry Couch Jagoe (father):**

**Residence - 1 Rialto Terrace South Circular Road - March 12, 1865**

$$\text{December 11, 1866}$$

**Occupation - Clerk of Works Royal Engineer Department - March 12, 1865**

$$\text{December 11, 1866}$$

- James Jagoe & Anne Hayes

  o Samuel Jagoe – bapt. 21 Nov 1850 (Baptism, **Drimoleague Parish (RC)**)

**Samuel Jagoe (son):**

**Remarks at Birth - bastard**

- John Jagoe & Anne Cadogan

  o Mary Jagoe – bapt. 26 Apr 1815 (Baptism, **Skibbereen (Creagh & Sullon) Parish (RC)**)

  o Elizabeth Jagoe – bapt. 1 Dec 1817 (Baptism, **Skibbereen (Creagh & Sullon) Parish (RC)**)

  o Patrick Jagoe – bapt. 24 Sep 1820 (Baptism, **Skibbereen (Creagh & Sullon) Parish (RC)**)

  o Jane Jagoe – bapt. 4 Apr 1823 (Baptism, **Skibbereen (Creagh & Sullon) Parish (RC)**)

  o Ellen Jagoe – bapt. 3 Mar 1826 (Baptism, **Skibbereen (Creagh & Sullon) Parish (RC)**)

  o Michael Jagoe – bapt. 5 Oct 1830 (Baptism, **Skibbereen (Creagh & Sullon) Parish (RC)**)

**John Jagoe (father):**

**Residence - Bridgetown - April 26, 1815**

$$\text{December 1, 1817}$$

$$\text{September 24, 1820}$$

$$\text{April 4, 1823}$$

$$\text{March 3, 1826}$$

# Jagoe Surname Ireland: 1600s to 1900s

- John Jagoe & Elizabeth Sullivan

  o Alice Jagoe – bapt. 4 Jan 1855 (Baptism, **Cork - South Parish (RC)**)

  o John Jagoe – bapt. 13 Feb 1857 (Baptism, **Cork - South Parish (RC)**)

  o Abraham Joseph Jagoe – bapt. 21 Nov 1859 (Baptism, **Cork - South Parish (RC)**)

  o Elizabeth Jagoe – bapt. 21 Apr 1863 (Baptism, **Cork - South Parish (RC)**)

  o Mary Jagoe – b. 9 Dec 1866, bapt. 12 Dec 1866 (Baptism, **Cork - SS. Peter & Paul Parish (RC)**)

- John Jagoe & Honora Corcoran – Mar 1812 (Marriage, **Kilmurry Parish (RC)**)

  o Catherine Jagoe – bapt. 4 Aug 1814 (Baptism, **Kilmurry Parish (RC)**)

- John Jagoe & Honora Murphy

  o John Jagoe – bapt. 29 Jun 1829 (Baptism, **Enniskeane Parish (RC)**)

- John Jagoe & Jane Carthy

  o James Jagoe – bapt. 27 Aug 1869 (Baptism, **Muintervara Parish (RC)**)

**James Jagoe (father):**

**Residence - Droumreagh - August 27, 1869**

- John Jagoe & Julia Brien – 10 Feb 1835 (Marriage, **Dunmanway Parish (RC)**)

  o Patrick Jagoe – bapt. 29 Mar 1836 (Baptism, **Dunmanway Parish (RC)**)

  o Ellen Jagoe – bapt. 19 May 1837 (Baptism, **Dunmanway Parish (RC)**)

  o Edward Jagoe – bapt. 19 Nov 1838 (Baptism, **Dunmanway Parish (RC)**)

  o Charles Jagoe – bapt. 20 Jun 1840 (Baptism, **Dunmanway Parish (RC)**)

  o John Jagoe – bapt. 4 Mar 1842 (Baptism, **Dunmanway Parish (RC)**)

  o Catherine Jagoe – bapt. 10 Aug 1844 (Baptism, **Dunmanway Parish (RC)**)

  o Mary Jagoe – bapt. 10 Aug 1844 (Baptism, **Dunmanway Parish (RC)**)

# Hurst

John Jagoe (father):

Residence - Monireague - February 10, 1835

Cullinagh - May 19, 1837

Pookeen - March 29, 1836

November 19, 1838

June 20, 1840

March 4, 1842

August 10, 1844

Julia Brien (mother):

Residence - Monireague - February 10, 1835

- John Jagoe & Julia Sullivan – 9 Feb 1875 (Marriage, **Innishannon Parish** (RC))

- John Jagoe & Margaret Corcoran

  o Joseph Jagoe – bapt. 20 Jun 1813 (Baptism, **Kilmurry Parish** (RC))

- John Jagoe & Margaret Hussey – 16 Nov 1828 (Marriage, **Bandon Parish** (RC))

- John Jagoe & Margaret Shea

  o John Jagoe – bapt. 24 Jan 1836 (Baptism, **Innishannon Parish** (RC))

- John Jagoe & Mary Beamish – 22 Feb 1868 (Marriage, **Dunmanway Parish** (RC))

- John Jagoe & Unknown

  o Patrick Jagoe & Abigail McGowan – 7 Jan 1889 (Marriage, **Tralee Parish** (RC))

Patrick Jagoe (son):

Residence - Tralee - January 7, 1889

Abigail McGowan, daughter of Daniel McGowan (daughter-in-law):

Residence - Tralee - January 7, 1889

# Jagoe Surname Ireland: 1600s to 1900s

- Jonathan Jagoe & Unknown

  - Charles Boyle Jagoe (1st Marriage) & Elizabeth Power – 6 Feb 1853 (Marriage, **St. George Parish**)

**Signatures:**

**Charles Boyle Jagoe (son):**

    Residence -82 Grafton Street, St. Anne Parish - February 6, 1853

    Occupation - Gentleman - February 6, 1853

**Elizabeth Power, daughter of James Power (daughter-in-law):**

    Residence - 71 Phibsboro Road - February 6, 1853

**James Power (father):**

    Occupation - Clerk

**Jonathan Jagoe (father):**

    Occupation - Merchant

  - Charles Boyle Jagoe (2nd Marriage) & Mary Newman – 16 Aug 1859 (Marriage, **St. Peter Parish**)

**Signatures:**

# Hurst

- Charles William Jagoe – b. 4 Oct 1860, bapt. 25 Nov 1860 (Baptism, **St. Peter Parish**)

- Walter Charles Jagoe & Mary Elizabeth O'Reilly – 7 Mar 1888 (Marriage, **St. Andrew Parish**)

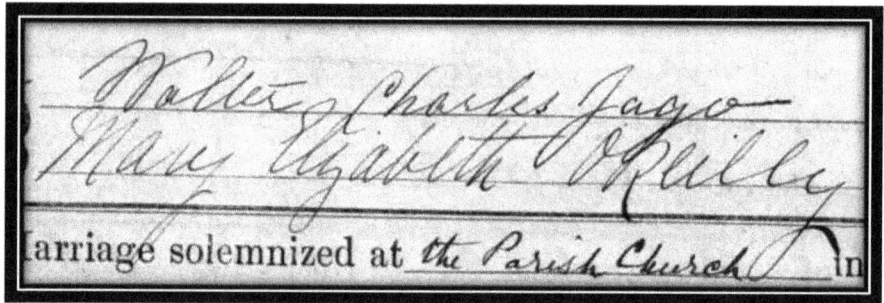

Signatures:

Walter Charles Jagoe (son):

Residence - 64 York Street, Belfast - March 7, 1888

Occupation - Dentist - March 7, 1888

Mary Elizabeth O'Reilly, daughter of Dennis P. O'Reilly (daughter-in-law):

Residence - 16 Eustace Street - March 7, 1888

Dennis P. O'Reilly (father):

Signature:

Occupation - Draper

Charles Boyle Jagoe (father):

Occupation - Draper

# Jagoe Surname Ireland: 1600s to 1900s

Wedding Witnesses:

Dennis P. O'Reilly & William H. Jagoe

Signatures:

Charles Boyle Jagoe (son):

    Residence - 2 Albert Place - August 16, 1859

           46 lower Camden Street - November 25, 1860

    Occupation - Esquire - August 16, 1859

           Accountant - November 25, 1860

    Relationship Status at Marriage - widow

Mary Newman, daughter of George Newman (daughter-in-law):

    Residence - 5th Grantham Street - August 16, 1859

George Newman (father):

    Occupation - Esquire

Jonathan Jagoe (father):

    Occupation - Merchant

Wedding Witnesses:

William Telford & Jane Newman

Signatures:

# Hurst

- Lewis Jagoe & Jane Jagoe

  o Agnes Jagoe – b. 7 May 1876, bapt. 8 Jul 1876 (Baptism, **Beggar's Bush Barracks Parish**)

**Lewis Jagoe (father):**

**Residence - Beggar's Bush Barracks - July 8, 1876**

**Occupation - Sergeant 93ʳᵈ Highlanders - July 8, 1876**

- Patrick Jagoe & Catherine Connolly – 22 Sep 1852 (Marriage, **Cork - South Parish** (RC))

  o Catherine Margaret Jagoe – bapt. 13 Oct 1858 (Baptism, **Cork - South Parish** (RC))

- Patrick Jagoe & Catherine Kelly

  o Patrick Jagoe – bapt. 3 Apr 1792 (Baptism, **Bantry Parish** (RC))

- Patrick Jagoe & Elizabeth Rochford – 25 Sep 1841 (Marriage, **Cork - South Parish** (RC))

- Patrick Jagoe & Ellen Hurley

  o Mary Jagoe – bapt. 18 Dec 1819 (Baptism, **Kilmurry Parish** (RC))

  o Patrick Jagoe – bapt. 28 Jul 1824 (Baptism, **Kilmurry Parish** (RC))

  o John Jagoe – bapt. 14 Oct 1827 (Baptism, **Kilmurry, Moviddy, Kilbonane, & Cannavee Parish** (RC))

**Patrick Jagoe (father):**

**Residence - Castlemore - July 28, 1824**

**October 14, 1827**

- Patrick Jagoe & Ellen Hurley – 6 Feb 1853 (Marriage, **Skibbereen & Rath Parish** (RC))

  o Mary A. Jagoe – bapt. 27 Feb 1855 (Baptism, **Skibbereen (Creagh & Sullon) Parish** (RC))

  o John Jagoe – bapt. 8 Jun 1856 (Baptism, **Skibbereen (Creagh & Sullon) Parish** (RC))

  o Anne Jagoe – bapt. 26 Feb 1860 (Baptism, **Skibbereen (Creagh & Sullon) Parish** (RC))

  o Richard Jagoe – bapt. 14 Aug 1862 (Baptism, **Skibbereen (Creagh & Sullon) Parish** (RC))

  o Patrick Jagoe – bapt. 22 Nov 1864 (Baptism, **Skibbereen (Creagh & Sullon) Parish** (RC))

# Jagoe Surname Ireland: 1600s to 1900s

**Patrick Jagoe (father):**

Residence - Upper Bridgetown - February 27, 1855

Bridgetown - June 8, 1856

February 26, 1860

August 14, 1862

Skibbereen - November 22, 1864

- Patrick Jagoe & Mary Murphy

  o Unknown Jagoe – bapt. 1 Aug 1824 (Baptism, **Cork - South Parish (RC)**)

- Patrick Jagoe & Unknown

  o Michael Jagoe & Elizabeth Price – 5 Jan 1862 (Marriage, **Tralee Parish (RC)**)

    ▪ James Jagoe – b. 9 Dec 1862, bapt. 14 Dec 1862 (Baptism, **Tralee Parish (RC)**)

    ▪ Margaret Jagoe – b. 3 Sep 1865, bapt. 24 Sep 1865 (Baptism, **Tralee Parish (RC)**)

**Michael Jagoe (son):**

Residence - Tralee - January 5, 1862

December 14, 1862

Moyderwell - September 24, 1865

**Elizabeth Price, daughter of William Price (daughter-in-law):**

Residence - Tralee - January 5, 1862

- Samuel Jagoe & Margaret Fitzgerald – 4 Jul 1826 (Marriage, **Cork - South Parish (RC)**)

  o William Jagoe – bapt. 20 Jan 1824 (Baptism, **Cork - South Parish (RC)**)

  o Margaret Jagoe – bapt. 4 Jun 1831 (Baptism, **Cork - South Parish (RC)**)

  o Joseph Jagoe – bapt. Nov 1833 (Baptism, **Cork - South Parish (RC)**)

- Samuel Jagoe & Peg Keragh

  o Patrick Jagoe – bapt. 18 Jun 1859 (Baptism, **Drimoleague Parish (RC)**)

**Patrick Jagoe (son):**

Remarks at Birth - bastard

# Hurst

- Thomas Jagoe & Mary Jagoe

  - Eleanor Jagoe – bapt. 13 Mar 1709 (Baptism, **St. John Parish**)

## Thomas Jagoe (father):

### Occupation - Merchant - March 13, 1709

- Thomas Jagoe & Susan Lambert

  - Sally Jagoe – bapt. 21 Sep 1835 (Baptism, **Drimoleague Parish** (RC))

- William Jagoe & Honora Sullivan

  - Felix Jagoe – bapt. 12 Jan 1840 (Baptism, **Drimoleague Parish** (RC))

- William Jagoe & Joan Daly

  - Richard Jagoe – bapt. Apr 1840 (Baptism, **Dunmanway Parish** (RC))

- William Jagoe & Catherine Atkins – 17 Nov 1860 (Baptism, **Kilmacabea Parish** (RC))

## Catherine Atkins (wife):

### Residence - Leap - November 17, 1860

- William Jagoe & Mary Brien

  - Daniel Jagoe – bapt. 31 Jan 1831 (Baptism, **Drimoleague Parish** (RC))

- William Jagoe & Unknown

  - William Henry Jagoe & Leticia White – 12 Dec 1890 (Marriage, **St. George Parish**)

**Signatures:**

# Jagoe Surname Ireland: 1600s to 1900s

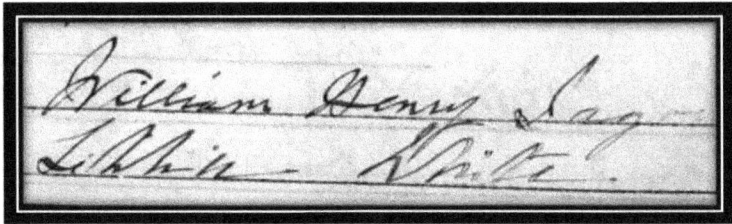

**Signatures (Marriage):**

**William Henry Jagoe (son):**

    Residence - 1 Warrenpoint Clontarf, Co. Dublin - December 12, 1890

    Occupation - Medical Doctor - December 12, 1890

**Leticia White, daughter of James White (daughter-in-law):**

    Residence - 2 Belvidere Avenue - December 12, 1890

**James White (father):**

    Occupation - Esquire

**William Jagoe (father):**

    Occupation - Esquire

# Individual Births/Baptisms

- Mary Anne Jagoe – bapt. 29 May 1839 (Baptism, **Drimoleague Parish (RC)**)

# Individual Burials

- Henry Jagoe – b. 1697, bur. 26 Dec 1745 (Burial, **St. Werburgh Parish**)

Henry Jagoe (deceased):

   Residence - Castle Street - Before December 26, 1745

   Age at Death - 48 years

   Cause of Death - Decay

- Sarah Jagoe – b. 1691, bur. 19 Oct 1741 (Burial, **St. Werburgh Parish**)

Sarah Jagoe (deceased):

   Residence - Castle Yard - Before October 19, 1741

   Age at Death - 50 years

   Cause of Death - fever

- Thomas Jagoe – b. 1685, bur. 30 Nov 1734 (Burial, **St. Werburgh Parish**)

Thomas Jagoe (deceased):

   Residence - Hoey's Alley - Before November 30, 1734

   Age at Death - 49 years

   Cause of Death - consumption

# Individual Marriages

- Anne Jagoe & Dennis McCarthy

  - Catherine McCarthy – bapt. 9 Mar 1807 (Baptism, **Tracton Abbey Parish** (RC))

  - Margaret McCarthy – bapt. 6 Feb 1810 (Baptism, **Tracton Abbey Parish** (RC))

  - John McCarthy – bapt. 31 Jan 1812 (Baptism, **Tracton Abbey Parish** (RC))

  - Michael McCarthy – bapt. 21 Jan 1813 (Baptism, **Tracton Abbey Parish** (RC))

  - Dennis McCarthy – bapt. 30 Jun 1817 (Baptism, **Tracton Abbey Parish** (RC))

  - Mary McCarthy – bapt. 4 Mar 1821 (Baptism, **Tracton Abbey Parish** (RC))

  - Julia McCarthy – bapt. 11 Feb 1824 (Baptism, **Tracton Abbey Parish** (RC))

- Catherine Jagoe & Darby Donovan

  - Patrick Donovan – bapt. 27 Mar 1838 (Baptism, **Drimoleague Parish** (RC))

- Catherine Jagoe & Jeremiah Donovan – 7 Feb 1837 (Marriage, **Drimoleague Parish** (RC))

  - Jeremiah Donovan – bapt. 11 Jan 1841 (Baptism, **Drimoleague Parish** (RC))

  - Joan Donovan – bapt. 24 Jan 1844 (Baptism, **Drimoleague Parish** (RC))

**Catherine Jagoe (mother):**

**Occupation - Servant - February 7, 1837**

- Catherine Jagoe & Michael Connelly

  - Patrick Connelly – bapt. 13 Apr 1850 (Baptism, **Kilmacabea Parish** (RC))

- Catherine Jagoe & Richard Donovan

  - Mary Donovan – bapt. 25 Mar 1844 (Baptism, **Bantry Parish** (RC))

- Catherine Jagoe & Thomas Hurley – 5 Mar 1871 (Marriage, **Dunmanway Parish** (RC))

  - Patrick Hurley – bapt. 17 Mar 1872 (Baptism, **Dunmanway Parish** (RC))

# Jagoe Surname Ireland: 1600s to 1900s

- Catherine Jagoe & Timothy Donovan

  o Catherine Donovan – bapt. 14 Oct 1848 (Baptism, **Drimoleague Parish** (RC))

- Catherine Jagoe & Timothy Sullivan

  o Mary Sullivan – bapt. 17 Dec 1807 (Baptism, **Kilmurry Parish** (RC))

  o Cornelius (C o r n e l i u s) Sullivan – bapt. Apr 1811 (Baptism, **Kilmurry Parish** (RC))

  o Patrick Sullivan – bapt. 31 Jul 1819 (Baptism, **Kilmurry Parish** (RC))

- Eleanor Jagoe & John Dwyer – 2 Apr 1796 (Marriage, **St. Andrew Parish** (RC))

- Eleanor Jagoe & William Streeter – 4 Oct 1716 (Marriage, **St. John Parish**)

- Elizabeth Jagoe & Edward Forbes

  o Richard Forbes – bapt. 15 May 1842 (Baptism, **Drimoleague Parish** (RC))

- Elizabeth Jagoe & Harold Wilkinson

  o Francis Wilkinson – bapt. Nov 1822 (Baptism, **Kilmichael Parish** (RC))

- Elizabeth Jagoe & Henry Wilkinson

  o Abraham Wilkinson – bapt. May 1835 (Baptism, **Kilmichael Parish** (RC))

**Henry Wilkinson (father):**

**Residence - Dromleigh - May 1835**

- Elizabeth Jagoe & James Donovan – 5 Feb 1839 (Marriage, **Dunmanway Parish** (RC))

  o Julia Donovan – bapt. 27 Jan 1840 (Baptism, **Dunmanway Parish** (RC))

  o Catherine Donovan – bapt. 3 Sep 1842 (Baptism, **Drimoleague Parish** (RC))

  o Michael Donovan – bapt. 6 Jul 1845 (Baptism, **Drimoleague Parish** (RC))

**Elizabeth Jagoe (mother):**

**Residence - Clounties - February 5, 1839**

**James Donovan (father):**

**Residence - Clounties - February 5, 1839**

**Kilronan - January 27, 1840**

# Hurst

- Elizabeth Jagoe & Jeremiah Dempsey

  o Daniel Dempsey – bapt. 13 Mar 1855 (Baptism, **Kilmacabea Parish (RC)**)

  o Ellen Dempsey – bapt. 13 Apr 1862 (Baptism, **Kilmacabea Parish (RC)**)

  o James Dempsey – bapt. 31 Aug 1864 (Baptism, **Kilmacabea Parish (RC)**)

- Elizabeth Jagoe & Jeremiah Regan – 8 Feb 1844 (Marriage, **Kinsale Parish (RC)**)

  o Elizabeth Regan – bapt. 12 Sep 1848 (Baptism, **Kinsale Parish (RC)**)

**Jeremiah Regan (father):**

**Residence - Glen - February 8, 1844**

- Elizabeth Jagoe & Matthew Neville

  o Ellen Neville – bapt. 4 Aug 1850 (Baptism, **Kilmichael Parish (RC)**)

  o Mary Neville – bapt. 25 Mar 1852 (Baptism, **Kilmichael Parish (RC)**)

  o Jane Neville – bapt. 8 Aug 1853 (Baptism, **Kilmichael Parish (RC)**)

  o Maurice Neville – bapt. 15 Aug 1855 (Baptism, **Kilmichael Parish (RC)**)

  o Margaret Neville – bapt. 4 Oct 1857 (Baptism, **Kilmichael Parish (RC)**)

  o Elizabeth Neville – bapt. 11 Oct 1863 (Baptism, **Kilmichael Parish (RC)**)

**Matthew Neville (father):**

**Residence - Inchinashingane - August 4, 1850**

**March 25, 1852**

**August 8, 1853**

**August 15, 1855**

**October 4, 1857**

- Elizabeth Jagoe & William Geany

  o Catherine Geany – bapt. 2 Mar 1841 (Baptism, **Skibbereen (Creagh & Sullon) Parish (RC)**)

- Ellen Jagoe & John Donovan

  o Cornelius (C o r n e l i u s) Donovan – bapt. 5 Jul 1857 (Baptism, **Drimoleague Parish (RC)**)

# Jagoe Surname Ireland: 1600s to 1900s

- Ellen Jagoe & John McCarthy – 27 Feb 1838 (Marriage, **Dunmanway Parish** (RC))

  o Bridget McCarthy – bapt. 1 Feb 1839 (Baptism, **Drimoleague Parish** (RC))

  o Honora McCarthy – bapt. 17 Mar 1841 (Baptism, **Drimoleague Parish** (RC))

  o John McCarthy – bapt. 26 Jul 1844 (Baptism, **Drimoleague Parish** (RC))

  o Ellen McCarthy – bapt. 6 May 1846 (Baptism, **Drimoleague Parish** (RC))

  o Patrick McCarthy – bapt. 12 Mar 1849 (Baptism, **Drimoleague Parish** (RC))

  o Mary McCarthy – bapt. 19 Jul 1851 (Baptism, **Drimoleague Parish** (RC))

  o John McCarthy – bapt. 7 May 1854 (Baptism, **Drimoleague Parish** (RC))

**Ellen Jagoe (mother):**

**Residence - Pookeen - February 27, 1838**

**John McCarthy (father):**

**Residence - Pookeen - February 27, 1838**

- Ellen Jagoe & John Wilkinson

  o John Wilkinson – bapt. 15 Jun 1826 (Baptism, **Kilmichael Parish** (RC))

**John Wilkinson (father):**

**Residence - Dromleigh - June 15, 1826**

- Ellen Jagoe & Ned Fleming

  o Sally Fleming – bapt. Apr 1827 (Baptism, **Kilbrittain Parish** (RC))

- Ellen Jagoe & Timothy Buckly – 15 Aug 1848 (Marriage, **Cork - South Parish** (RC))

  o Ellen Buckly – bapt. 19 May 1852 (Baptism, **Cork - South Parish** (RC))

- Grace Jagoe & Jeremiah Neil

  o Julia Neil – bapt. 5 Oct 1828 (Baptism, **Cork - South Parish** (RC))

# Hurst

- Hester Jagoe & Patrick Desmond – 10 Feb 1839 (Marriage, **Bantry Parish** (RC))

  - Jane Mary Desmond – bapt. 15 Dec 1839 (Baptism, **Bantry Parish** (RC))

  - Henry Gerald Desmond – bapt. 1 Dec 1841 (Baptism, **Bantry Parish** (RC))

  - Ellen Desmond – bapt. 9 Nov 1843 (Baptism, **Bantry Parish** (RC))

  - Timothy Desmond – bapt. 22 Feb 1846 (Baptism, **Bantry Parish** (RC))

  - Patrick Desmond – bapt. 22 Feb 1846 (Baptism, **Bantry Parish** (RC))

- Mary Jagoe & Alexander Gill

  - James Gill – bapt. 4 Feb 1830 (Baptism, **Dunmanway Parish** (RC))

### Alexander Gill (father):

### Residence - Ballybee - February 4, 1830

- Mary Jagoe & Daniel Kingston – 13 Feb 1836 (Marriage, **Dunmanway Parish** (RC))

  - William Kingston – bapt. 11 Feb 1837 (Baptism, **Drimoleague Parish** (RC))

  - John Kingston – bapt. 13 Feb 1839 (Baptism, **Drimoleague Parish** (RC))

  - Darby Kingston – bapt. 22 Mar 1842 (Baptism, **Drimoleague Parish** (RC))

  - Mary Kingston – bapt. 22 Mar 1846 (Baptism, **Drimoleague Parish** (RC))

### Mary Jagoe (mother):

### Residence - Pookeen - February 13, 1836

### Daniel Kingston (father):

### Residence - Pookeen - February 13, 1836

- Mary Jagoe & Dennis McCarthy – 27 Nov 1847 (Marriage, **Kilmurry, Moviddy, Kilbonane, & Cannavee Parish** (RC))

  - Mary McCarthy – bapt. 23 Oct 1848 (Baptism, **Ballinhassig Parish** (RC))

  - Catherine McCarthy – bapt. 30 Jan 1858 (Baptism, **Ballinhassig Parish** (RC))

  - Honora McCarthy – bapt. 5 Mar 1862 (Baptism, **Ballinhassig Parish** (RC))

# Jagoe Surname Ireland: 1600s to 1900s

- Mary Jagoe & Jeffery Gibton – 28 Jan 1738 (Marriage, **St. Nicholas Within Parish**)

- Mary Jagoe & John Gardner – 5 Jun 1745 (Marriage, **St. Andrew Parish**)

- Mary Anne Jagoe & Charles McCarthy – 6 Jul 1837 (Marriage, **Drimoleague Parish (RC)**)

  o Charles McCarthy – bapt. 16 Feb 1838 (Baptism, **Drimoleague Parish (RC)**)

  o Honora McCarthy – bapt. 10 Jul 1839 (Baptism, **Drimoleague Parish (RC)**)

  o Catherine McCarthy – bapt. 21 Feb 1841 (Baptism, **Drimoleague Parish (RC)**)

  o Mary McCarthy – bapt. 30 Sep 1842 (Baptism, **Drimoleague Parish (RC)**)

  o Ellen McCarthy – bapt. 28 Dec 1844 (Baptism, **Drimoleague Parish (RC)**)

  o James McCarthy – bapt. 8 Aug 1847 (Baptism, **Drimoleague Parish (RC)**)

- Rebecca Ellen Jagoe & Nicholas Haly Coppinger

  o Rebecca Coppinger – bapt. 12 Sep 1799 (Baptism, **Cork - South Parish (RC)**)

  o Michael Francis Haly Coppinger – bapt. 13 Oct 1800 (Baptism, **Cork - South Parish (RC)**)

  o Frances Coppinger – bapt. 23 Jun 1803 (Baptism, **Cork - South Parish (RC)**)

**Nicholas Coppinger (father):**

**Residence - Cold Harbor - October 13, 1800**

**Warren's Quay - June 23, 1803**

**Occupation - Esquire - September 12, 1799**

**October 13, 1800**

**June 23, 1803**

- Ursula Jagoe & Thomas McNamara – 17 Jun 1862 (Marriage, **Cork - South Parish (RC)**)

  o Mary McNamara – bapt. 27 Dec 1861 (Baptism, **Cork - South Parish (RC)**)

# Name Variations

**Includes Latin and Abbreviated forms of names found in the original documents.**

Abigail = Abigale, Abigall

Anne = Ann, Anna, Annae

Bartholomew = Barth, Bartholmeus, Bartholomeo

Bridget = Birgis, Brigid, Brigida, Bridgit

Catherine = Catharine, Catharina, Catharinae, Catherina, Cath, Catha, Cathae, Cathe, Cathn, Kate

Charles = Carolus, Charls, Chas

Christopher = Christoph

Daniel = Danielem, Danielis

Edward = Ed, Edwd

Eleanor = Eleo, Eleonora, Elinor, Ellenor

Elizabeth = Betty, Elisa, Elisabeth, Eliz, Eliza, Elizab, Elizh, Elizth

Ellen = Elena, Ellena

Emily= Emilia

Esther = Essie, Ester

Francis = Fransicum

George = Geo, Georg, Georgius

Grace = Gratiae

Gulielmo = Guil, Guillelmi, Gulielmum, Guillelmus, Gulmi

Harold = Harry

Helen = Helena

Honor = Hanora, Honora

# Jagoe Surname Ireland: 1600s to 1900s

James = Jacobi, Jacobus, Jas

Jane = Joanna

Jeanne = Jeannae, Joannae

Joan = Johanna, Joney

John = Jno, Joannem, Joannes, Johannis

Joseph = Jos

Juliana = Julian

Leticia = Letitia, Lettice, Letticia

Lewis = Louis

Luke = Lucas

Margaret = Margarita, Margaritae, Margeret, Marget, Margt

Martha = Marthae

Mary = Maria, My

Mary Anne = Marianna, Marianne, Maryanne

Michael = Michaelis, Michl

Patrick = Pat, Patt, Patk, Patricii, Patricius

Peter = Petri

Richard = Ricardi, Ricardus, Rich, Richd

Robert = Roberti

Rose = Rosa, Rosae

Samuel = Samuelis

Thomas = Thom, Thomae, Thoms, Thos, Ths

Timothy = Timotheus, Timy

Valentine = Val, Valentinae, Valentinus

William = Wil, Will, Willm, Wm

# Notes

# Notes

# Notes

# Notes

# Notes

# Notes

# Index

# Jagoe Surname Ireland: 1600s to 1900s

**Fitzgerald**

**Jagoe**

# Jagoe Surname Ireland: 1600s to 1900s

# About The Author

Donovan Hurst graduated from San Diego State University with a Bachelor of Arts in the major field of studies of History and a minor in the field of studies of Anthropology. He is a current member of The General Society of Mayflower Descendants and has been conducting genealogical research for over 10 years tracing back his ancestors to their ancestral homelands in Denmark, England, France, Germany, Ireland, Norway, and Scotland.

www.ingramcontent.com/pod-product-compliance
Lightning Source LLC
Chambersburg PA
CBHW081204270326
41930CB00014B/3289